Encountering God

PSALMS
VOLUME I

New Community Bible Study Series

Old Testament
    Exodus: Journey toward God
    1 and 2 Samuel: Growing a Heart for God
    Nehemiah: Overcoming Challenges
    Psalms Vol. 1: Encountering God
    Psalms Vol. 2: Life-Changing Lessons
    Daniel: Pursuing Integrity

New Testament
    Sermon on the Mount 1: Connect with God
    Sermon on the Mount 2: Connect with Others
    The Lord's Prayer: Praying with Power
    Parables: Imagine Life God's Way
    Luke: Lessons from Jesus
    Acts: Build Community
    Romans: Find Freedom
    2 Corinthians: Serving from the Heart
    Philippians: Run the Race
    Colossians: Discover the New You
    James: Live Wisely
    1 Peter: Stand Strong
    1 John: Love Each Other
    Revelation: Experience God's Power

BILL HYBELS

WITH KEVIN & SHERRY HARNEY

New Community
KNOWING. LOVING. SERVING. CELEBRATING.

Encountering God

PSALMS
VOLUME I

Willow Creek Resources

ZONDERVAN.com/
AUTHORTRACKER
follow your favorite authors

ZONDERVAN®

Psalms Volume 1: Encountering God
Copyright © 2008 by Willow Creek Association

Requests for information should be addressed to:

Zondervan, *Grand Rapids, Michigan 49530*

ISBN 978-0-310-28052-1

Interior design by Sherri Hoffman

Printed in the United States of America

08 09 10 11 12 13 14 • 21 20 19 18 17 16 15 14 13 12 11 10 9 8 7 6 5 4 3 2 1

CONTENTS

God has created us for community. This need is built into the very fiber of our being, the DNA of our spirit. As Christians, our deepest desire is to see the truth of God's Word as it influences our relationships with others. We long for a dynamic encounter with God's Word, intimate closeness with his people, and radical transformation of our lives. But how can we accomplish those three difficult tasks?

The New Community Bible Study Series creates a place for all of this to happen. In-depth Bible study, community-building opportunities, and life-changing applications are all built into every session of this small group study guide.

How to Build Community

How do we build a strong, healthy Christian community? The whole concept for this study grows out of a fundamental understanding of Christian community that is dynamic and transformational. We believe that Christians don't simply gather to exchange doctrinal affirmations. Rather, believers are called by God to get into each other's lives. We are family, for better or for worse, and we need to connect with each other.

Community is not built through sitting in the same building and singing the same songs. It is forged in the fires of life. When we know each other deeply—the good, the bad, and the ugly—community is experienced. Community grows when we learn to rejoice with one another, celebrating life. Roots grow deep when we know we are loved by others and are free to extend love to them as well. Finally, community deepens and is built when we commit to serve each other and let others serve us. This process of doing ministry and humbly receiving the ministry of others is critical for healthy community life.

Build Community Through Knowing and Being Known

We all long to know others deeply and to be fully known by them. Although we might run from this level of intimacy at times, we all want to have people in our lives who trust us enough to disclose the deep and tender parts of themselves. In turn, we want to reveal some of our feelings, expressing them freely to people we trust.

The first section of each of these six studies creates a place for deep knowing and being known. Through serious reflection on the truth of Scripture, you will be invited to communicate parts of your heart and life with your small group members. You might even discover yourself opening parts of your heart that you have thus far kept hidden. The Bible study and discussion questions do not encourage surface conversation. The only way to go deep in knowing others and being known by them is to dig deep, and this takes work. Knowing others also takes trust—that you will honor each other and respect each other's confidences.

Build Community Through Celebrating and Being Celebrated

If you have not had a good blush recently, read a short book in the Bible called Song of Songs. It's a record of a bride and groom writing poetic and romantic love letters to each other. They are freely celebrating every conceivable aspect of each other's personality, character, and physical appearance. At one point the groom says, "You have made my heart beat fast with a single glance from your eyes." Song of Songs is a reckless celebration of life, love, and all that is good.

We need to recapture the joy and freedom of celebration. In every session of this study, your group will commit to celebrate together. Although there are many ways to express joy, we will let our expression of celebration come through prayer. In each session you will take time to come before the God of joy and celebrate who he is and what he is doing. You will also have opportunity to celebrate what God is doing in your life and the lives of those who are a part of your small group. You will become a community of affirmation, celebration, and joy through your prayer time together.

You will need to be sensitive during this time of prayer together. Not everyone feels comfortable praying with a group of people. Be aware that each person is starting at a different place in their freedom to pray in a group, so be patient. Seek to promote a warm and welcoming atmosphere where each person can stretch a little and learn what it means to be a community that celebrates with God in the center.

Build Community Through Loving and Being Loved

Unless we are exchanging deeply committed levels of love with a few people, we will die slowly on the inside. This is precisely why so many people feel almost nothing at all. If we don't learn to exchange love with family and friends, we will eventually grow numb and no longer believe love is even a possibility. This is not God's plan. He hungers for us to be loved and to give love to others. As a matter of fact, he wants this for us even more than we want it for ourselves.

Every session in this study will address the area of loving and being loved. You will be challenged, in your personal life and as a small group, to be intentional and consistent about building loving relationships. You will get practical tools and be encouraged to set measurable goals for giving and receiving love.

Build Community Through Serving and Being Served

Community is about serving and humbly allowing others to serve you. The single most stirring example of this is recorded in John 13, where Jesus takes the position of the lowest servant and washes the feet of his followers. He gives them a powerful example and then calls them to follow. Servanthood is at the very core of community. To sustain deep relationships over a long period of time, there must be humility and a willingness to serve each other.

At the close of each session will be a clear challenge to servanthood. As a group, and as individual followers of Christ, you will discover that community is built through serving others. You will also find that your own small group members will grow in their ability to extend service to your life.

Bible Study Basics

To get the most out of this study, you will need to prepare and participate. Here are some guidelines to help you.

Preparing for the Study

1. If possible, even if you are not the leader, look over each session before you meet, read the Bible passages, and answer the questions. The more you are prepared, the more you will gain from the study.
2. Begin your preparation with prayer. Ask God to help you understand the passage and apply it to your life.
3. A good modern translation, such as the New International Version, Today's New International Version, the New American Standard Bible, or the New Revised Standard Version, will give you the most help. Questions in this guide are based on the New International Version.
4. Read and reread the passages. You must know what the passage says before you can understand what it means and how it applies to you.
5. Write your answers in the spaces provided in the study guide. This will help you participate more fully in the discussion and will also help you personalize what you are learning.
6. Keep a Bible dictionary handy to look up unfamiliar words, names, or places.

Participating in the Study

1. Be willing to join in the discussion. The leader of the group will not be lecturing but will encourage people to discuss what they have learned in the passage. Plan to share what God has taught you during your preparation time.
2. Stick to the passages being studied. Base your answers on the verses being discussed rather than on outside authorities such as commentaries or your favorite author or speaker.

3. Try to be sensitive to the other members of the group. Listen attentively when they speak, and be affirming whenever you can. This will encourage more hesistant members of the group to participate.
4. Be careful not to dominate the discussion. By all means participate, but allow others to have equal time.
5. If you are a discussion leader or a participant who wants further insights, you will find additional comments in the Leader's Notes at the back of the book.

Psalms Vol. 1: Encountering God

Our understanding of the character of God has greater impact on us than we can begin to imagine. How we conceive of God determines almost everything else. When we study and meditate on the attributes of God, we gain a vision that begins to infiltrate our souls, our minds, and eventually, every aspect of our lives.

This vision of God determines whether we worship him with passion or apathy. It seems almost inconceivable that a Christian would not feel compelled to worship God, but this happens every day. In many cases the reason for this reluctance to go deep in worship is rooted in an inadequate concept of God. When we have a biblical and accurate understanding of our amazing God, both private and public worship begin to flow naturally.

A deficient concept of God is also the reason some followers of Jesus really don't pray much. If we see God as just a deity who got the universe started and does not care to be bothered by us puny humans, why take time to pray? But if we are convinced that God is personal and intimately involved in our lives, if we see him as a loving Father who is interested in the details of each day, prayer becomes a moment-by-moment conversation.

If we see God as the generous provider of all we need, we become liberal in our giving to God and others. When we realize God's nature is to love, we see ourselves, and those around us, through new eyes of compassion and care. The moment we realize God is all-powerful, we start trusting that he can meet any need we face. As we gain insight into the merciful heart of God, we feel compelled to serve the poor and care for the rejected in this world. In the moments we get glimpses of God's saving grace, we desire for all people to come to this amazing God and have their sins taken away, as far as the east is from the west.

The theologian R. C. Sproul is fond of saying that the single greatest need in the life of spiritual seekers is for them to come to a full understanding of who God is. Most nonbelieving people ignore or reject God because their view of him is a man-made caricature, and nothing like the God of the Bible. If these people could only come to understand and appreciate who God really is, they would be drawn to him.

Sproul also loves to point out that one of the greatest needs in the Christian community is exactly the same! Those who follow Christ need to know more about the true identity of our amazing God. The more we know about who God is, the more we will revere him, worship him, trust him, receive from him, and live for him.

The book of Psalms is one of the best sources of teaching on the character and nature of God. In Psalms we get a fresh vision of the attributes of the one, true, amazing God. As you walk through this series of studies, my prayer is that you encounter God in new ways, understanding how amazing he is, and then live for him with renewed passion.

God Is …

PSALM 103

When I visited Niagara Falls for the first time when I was in junior high school, I was not sure what to expect. Lots of water, I suppose. Driving up in our family car, my siblings and I tumbled out and ran over to the ledge and just stood there, our jaws hanging open. I had never seen anything like it before. The splendor of the Niagara Falls took my breath away. I was speechless. I thought to myself, *Nothing could top this!*

About ten years after my Niagara Falls experience I was on a plane in the middle of South America. We were somewhere over Brazil when the plane lost two of its four engines. We made an emergency landing and I discovered we were very close to Iguazu Falls. I had heard rumors that these falls were reported to be a hundred Niagara Falls. When I saw Iguazu Falls with my own eyes, I was in awe. I would have never dreamed it possible, but this experience trumped what I had seen ten years earlier. There I stood, feeling like a little kid again. My mouth was hanging open, and my eyes were big as saucers. I was amazed. Again I thought, *Nothing could top this!*

Now, years later, I still can't imagine more majestic waterfalls, but I know there is something even more amazing, more spectacular, and more awe-inspiring than any waterfall. It is God! We could stack up all the Seven Wonders of the Natural World and their splendor can't compare to the One who made every one of them.

A day will come when we will see God face-to-face and every wonder of this world will pale in comparison. We will fall on our knees and cry out, "Holy, holy, holy is the Lord God Almighty!" Until that day, we get glimpses and reminders of the greatness of the God we worship—and even a quick peek overwhelms us. This is what Psalm 103 does. It pulls back the veil of eternity and gives us a vision of the God we love.

Making the Connection

1. Describe a time you saw something amazing or awe-inspiring in creation.

How did what you saw give you a glimpse of God's creative power?

Knowing and Being Known

Read Psalm 103:1 – 22

2. In this psalm David tells us to "forget not all his benefits." What is one of "his benefits" you see in this psalm and what helps you remember this benefit?

3. Take time as a group to review Psalm 103 and draw a composite sketch of who God is based on it.

God is ... *love.* God is ... *understanding*

God is ... *compassionate* God is ... *a satisfying God gives us what we need*

God is ... *righteous* God is ... *all powerful*

God is ... *just and fair* God is ... *sovereign.*

God is ... *forgiving* God is ... *redeeming*

God is ... *healing* God is ... *ruler.*

gracious.

This list is not exhaustive, but it does give an awesome picture of the God we worship and follow. How have you experienced God as the one revealed in this psalm?

God Is Forgiving

God, by his very nature, is willing, even eager, to exonerate and pardon. When people repent of their sin with sincerity, God delights to forgive. This forgiveness is accomplished on the basis of who God is, not on our frantic efforts to prove ourselves worthy of his grace.

Sometimes we underestimate God's forgiving character. We keep punishing ourselves when we sin; we degrade ourselves; we heap penance on ourselves; we fixate on how unworthy we feel. The starting point of such behavior is the feeling that God does not want to forgive us and we must do something extraordinary to convince him to grant us grace.

Read Psalm 103:1–4, 10–12 and Ephesians 2:8–9

4. If God "forgives all our sins" and removes our transgressions "as far as the east is from the west," why do we sometimes feel the need to earn our way back into God's favor?

guilt.

unworthy of the gift

5. If we accept the Bible's teaching on the topic of forgiveness, if we really believe all our sins are forgiven, and they are as far away from us as the east is from the west, what implications does this have on the following:

- How God sees you right now (through the finished work of Jesus on the cross)

just as if it was never done.

- How you should see and treat yourself

- How you should view and treat someone who has wronged you but confessed this sin

Acts 17:24

God Is Compassionate and Loving

If I were pressed to limit my explanation of the character of God to one verse in the entire Bible, it would be Psalm 103:8. "The LORD is compassionate and gracious, slow to anger, abounding in love." God is compassionate and loving by nature. He has a tender heart toward people, a sympathetic spirit, the ability to feel pity. Just as a loving parent has compassion on his children, so God has compassion on those who fear him.

One day, years ago, I was driving in the car with my daughter, Shauna, who was just a little girl at the time. We were listening to a radio program about an orphanage. She was playing around with the power windows, so I said, off the cuff, "Hey, if you don't stop playing with those windows I will send you to that orphanage they're talking about." In retrospect, I'm confident that was not a top-ten moment in my parenting life, but we both knew I was just kidding. Her response was classic. She rolled her eyes and said, "If you dropped me off at the orphanage, you wouldn't last ten minutes." I said, "Yeah, you are probably right." She felt so secure in my love she could declare it with confidence. Maybe we should feel more of that same bold confidence when it comes to how we understand God's compassion and love for us as his children.

Read Psalm 103:4 – 5, 8, 11 – 18

6. One indicator of God's compassion for us as his beloved children is that he is slow to anger. What are some of the ways you have witnessed God's "slow to anger" heart of compassion?

   Ex. 34:6

   • Toward you personally?

   • Toward the church?

   • Toward our nation?

7. God has compassion on those who "fear him." What does it mean to "fear the Lord" in a healthy, life-giving way?

Those who honor God and order their lives in accordance with his will because of their reverence for him.
reverential trust in God and commitment to his revealed will (word)

8. Make a list of some ways healthy, loving parents look at and treat their child:

love them despite their faults
want what's good for them
treat them with respect (esp. as adults)

If God is truly a compassionate and loving Father, what implications does this have on how he views and wants to treat you?

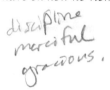
discipline
merciful
gracious.

God Is Sovereign

There is a throne in heaven, and God is sitting on it!

No matter what our eyes might see in this world, no matter how insecure we might feel, no matter what the news reports declare, God is on the throne and he still rules. He is in charge of this universe, sovereign over all kings, presidents, prime ministers, and even dictators. Don't ever be fooled into thinking that things are out of control. God's ways are higher than our ways and his thoughts are higher than our thoughts. Just because things don't make sense to us at times does not mean God has let the world slip out of his hands.

One day God will bring all of history to a close. He will crush Satan, separate himself from rebellious sinners, and embrace his children in his loving presence forever. In the meantime, we need to remember that he is sovereign. We can trust him.

Read Psalm 103:19–22

9. God is sovereign over our lives and what happens each day on this earth. Nothing in this world is outside of his control. How should this truth impact the way we view the evening news and the constant emphasis on all of the despair and pain in the world?

"I'm not scared."
"God is in control."
"Makes me rely on him."
"Reminds us that God is God."

10. God is sovereign over angels and the heavenly hosts. How might your outlook on each day's activities change if you lived with the awareness that there are angels doing God's bidding all around you?

not worry so much.
Surrender my day to Him,
surrender my children.

11. God is sovereign over creation. The mountains, oceans, trees, and valleys all declare God's majesty and power. He reveals himself in the beauty of his works. How have you experienced the power and sovereign majesty of God through creation's revelation of his presence?

Celebrating and Being Celebrated

Turn to the composite sketch you drew of God in question 3 (page 15). Using these attributes and characteristics, lift up prayers of praise and celebration for who God is and what this means for you as his follower.

Loving and Being Loved

One of the characteristics of God highlighted in this psalm is his forgiving nature. Jesus focused on this aspect of God's heart toward us and also called us to extend this same kind of grace to others. In the Lord's Prayer we read:

> Forgive us our debts,
>   as we also have forgiven our debtors. (Matthew 6:12)

As an act of love toward God, and toward others, identify a person who has wronged you and make a commitment to extend forgiveness to this person. It might take time, humility, honest conversations, and even tears, but it will be a gift to God, the person you forgive, and even to you.

Serving and Being Served

God is sovereign over all, including creation. In his rule over the world, God has given us responsibility. All the way back in the garden we read:

> So God created man in his own image,
>   in the image of God he created him;
>   male and female he created them.
> God blessed them and said to them, "Be fruitful and increase in number; fill the earth and subdue it. Rule over the fish of the sea and the birds of the air and over every living creature that moves on the ground." (Genesis 1:27–28)

The Lord God took the man and put him in the Garden of Eden to work it and take care of it. (Genesis 2:15)

Talk as a group about how you can serve God by caring for his creation. Identify steps you might take: as individuals, as a group, or as a church.

Only God

PSALM 62

Two little phrases can make all the difference between joy or sorrow, fulfillment or emptiness, and spiritual growth or stagnancy. These two phrases—just two words each—seem so close to each other, but they are radically different and can point your spiritual compass in divergent directions.

The phrases are:

"God only"
"God and"

A "God only" person finds their satisfaction, plain and simple, in God alone. They are aware of all that the world offers, but these things are not their focus or their first love. A consuming passion to love God, serve Jesus, and follow the leading of the Holy Spirit is the driving force of their life. Their joy is found in God. Their goals are shaped by a desire to walk in obedience to the teaching of the Bible. And serving God and people is their delight.

Conversely, a "God and" person is someone who tries to please God and people at the same time. This person attempts to lay up treasures in heaven and is consumed with the need to build an impressive portfolio here on earth. A "God and" person is someone who tries to enjoy the full blessings of God and indulge and experience the pleasures of sin, if he can somehow arrange for that to happen. This person lives with one foot in God's world and the other planted firmly in the things of the world.

King David, the writer of Psalm 62, walked both of these roads; he experienced the heights of a "God only" life and the depths of a "God and" life.

David's life changed drastically after his confrontation with Goliath. He experienced a meteoric rise to national attention. He went from an unknown, deeply spiritual shepherd lad to a folk hero; from Jesse's baby boy to the heir to the throne of Israel; from the pasture to the spotlight. As a shepherd he had time to himself, beautiful starlit evenings, and space for writing songs of worship to the Lord. During those years David learned what it meant to be a "God only" man. When David finally sat on the throne, things changed. The women loved him, money was no longer an issue, he was praised and adored. Something inside David changed and he became a "God and" man.

Making the Connection

1. What are some of the indicators or signs that a person is slipping into a "God and" lifestyle?

   running ahead of God's plans . seeking happiness in things
   seeking to please man .
   workaholic
   Sunday morning
   pleasures of sin
   put themselves first.
   self-indulgent

   Why is it so easy to be a "God and" Christ follower in our day and age?

   want more than we need.
   influenced by others

   time
   service

Knowing and Being Known

Read Psalm 62:1 – 8

2. What are some of the "God only" declarations in Psalm 62 and how might your faith deepen if you were a "God only" person in these areas of life?

"God only" declarations ...   *How my faith would deepen ...*

Soul rest in God alone → I wouldn't constantly
not shaken   be chasing after
                                                  not afraid, confident
my hope   solid, safe place
my rock   → run to him.
my salvation   communicate, stay
                                                       connected

3. Finish *one* of the statements below and explain why you concluded the statement the way you did:

- It is good to find rest in God, but it is real easy to find my rest (refreshment, place of peace) in ...

  vacation

- God is the one who protects his children, but another source of protection we often look to is ...

- Salvation is found in God, but lots of people still seem to feel the need to add something to what God has done. One example would be ...

  service

- When we walk close to Jesus we experience hope, but it is also easy to put my hope in ...

my children

"God and" Human Praise

Through a number of painful, embarrassing life experiences, David learned some lessons from the school of hard knocks. In Psalm 62 he desires to pass along that experience-earned wisdom to others, so they don't have to learn the hard way ... as he did. One of the things he warns about is falling in love with human praise:

> Lowborn men are but a breath,
> the highborn are but a lie;
> if weighed on a balance, they are nothing;
> together they are only a breath. (v. 9)

David is saying, "Living to impress other people is a dead-end road. Men's applause isn't what it's cracked up to be." David had heard the crowds chant praises of his victories. He knew how good it felt to be the object of everyone's attention, the big man on campus, a national folk hero. But he had come to realize that people come and go: they are "but a breath." It is God who never leaves!

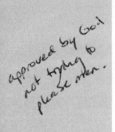
*approved by God,
not trying to
please others.*

Read Psalm 62:9 and 1 Thessalonians 2:1 – 6

4. "God and" individuals want to please God but they are also driven by a deep need to receive the praises of people. This can be a challenge for each of us from childhood through the waning years of our life. Choose *one* of the life situations below and identify some possible consequences:

    - A teenager who desperately wants the acceptance of his peers

      drugs

    - A university student who needs her professors to praise her and her work

      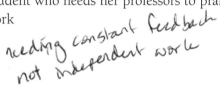
      *needing constant feedback
      not independent work*

    - A business person who will do anything for the boss's affirmation

      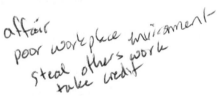
      *affair
      poor workplace environment
      steal others work
      take credit*

    - A pastor trying to please everyone in the congregation

      *nervous break-down
      constant defeat*

    - Make up your own scenario: _____

      _____

5. Tell about a time when your need to receive affirmation and praise from people became unhealthy.

If you had been living as a "God only" person at that time and your driving passion was to hear God say, "Well done, good and faithful servant," how might things have been different?

6. What are some of the attitude and lifestyle adjustments we can make to decrease our need to receive human praise?

do everything for the honor & glory of God.
healthy balance of work & play.

"God and" the Stuff of the World

David experienced a level of wealth that few people who walk this earth can even begin to imagine. As a king, if he wanted it, it was his! The stuff of the world was placed on a golden platter and offered to him day after day. In this psalm David also warns about the dangers of a "God and" life when it comes to material possessions:

> Do not trust in extortion
>   or take pride in stolen goods;
> though your riches increase,
>   do not set your heart on them. (v. 10)

(cont.)

27

Near the end of his life, David could have easily looked back and said, "When I was a penniless shepherd boy I felt secure in God alone. I had very little, but everything I needed. I felt content and satisfied. When I became king and the money started to roll in, things changed. Slowly but surely, my security came from 'God and' my treasure chest, 'God and' my earning power, 'God and' my financial wizardry, 'God and' my royal position. Surprisingly, the 'God and' approach ended up eroding my sense of security, protection, contentedness, and satisfaction."

Read Psalm 62:10 and Matthew 6:24 – 34

7. What do these passages teach you about living a "God and" life when it comes to material possessions?

   What do these passages say that affirms those who seek to live a "God only" life when it comes to our perspective on material goods?

8. Describe a time when you struggled with being a "God and" person drawn to put your trust in material things.

   How did this impact your relationship with God?

9. What is one lesson you have learned about how to live a life built on trust in God and not the accumulation of wealth and things?

Sliding from a "God Only" to a "God and" Life

It happened to David, it has happened to countless people through the centuries, and it can happen to us. It is painfully easy to slide from a "God only" life to a "God and" life. Slowly, almost imperceptibly, it happens. Inch by inch, choice by choice, attitude by attitude, we change. It can happen to the most committed and passionate followers of Jesus ... remember, it happened to David and he was called "a man after God's heart."

Sometimes slowing down and remembering where we have been can help us gain clarity on where we are today. Reflect honestly on each of the statements below. Allow yourself to:

- Remember when thoughts of God consumed your mind and doing his will was on the front burner of your heart at all times.
- Remember when you were convinced that God could do anything and that his power was sufficient for all your needs.
- Remember when being used for the purposes of Jesus brought you unspeakable satisfaction and you looked for ways to serve him each day.
- Remember when you looked for opportunities to walk across a room to meet a stranger or extend a hand to a person just because you wanted them to know God's love for them.
- Remember when you felt so ridiculously secure in God's faithfulness that you would have given away your car, house, boat, truck, or clothes because you were absolutely convinced that God held you in the palm of his hand.

Read Psalm 62:11 – 12

10. Tell about a season of your life when you were a passionate and reckless "God only" Christ follower.

What is one thing you can do to reclaim some of that radical devotion?

11. How can your group members encourage you and cheer you on as you seek to take steps toward being a more devoted "God only" person?

Celebrating and Being Celebrated

Sometimes, when it comes to material things, we end up focusing on the gift and forget the giver. One of the ways to adjust our perspective is remembering the Giver of every good gift. Take time as a group to pray, thanking God for all of his many provisions. Celebrate God's generosity and goodness by lifting up thanks for specific material things you have. But, in each case, with each prayer, acknowledge that this "gift" has a giver. Let your focus be on God, who provides so freely and graciously.

Loving and Being Loved

Take time to affirm where you have seen a "God only" attitude or lifestyle in other members of your group. Share these openly and boldly.

Serving and Being Served

If you have young children, grandchildren, or nieces and nephews, consider this unique service project. Like David, the best time to learn to be a "God only" person is when you are young, before the temptations of pleasing people and loving the material things of this world become so strong.

Consider having a one-on-one time with a young person who is dear to you and share about times in your life when you discovered the joys of being a "God only" person. Also, be honest about times when the praises of people or the love of things got in the way of your relationship with God. Give them a gentle challenge to do all they can to grow up as "God only" people, with a single-hearted attitude toward him.

God in Crisis

PSALM 46

Suddenly and swiftly, without advanced warning, the earth trembles, mountains come crashing down, and the seas rage. An already fragile-feeling human being can only surmise that the whole world is caving in. Sometimes our relational world, or our emotional world, our financial world, or even our spiritual world can feel like it is about to go through a cataclysmic upheaval ... and we have a sense that there is nothing we can do about it.

An unexpected phone call comes. A letter that looks the same as every other letter shows up in our mailbox. A knock on the door that sounded friendly enough. Then, in a matter of seconds, upon receiving the information, your whole world feels like it is caving in on you. Most of us have faced moments like this.

For some, the catastrophe was health related. Just a regular checkup that turned out to be anything but regular; just a little "complication" with your newborn baby; just a minor pain that turned out to be much more serious. Sometimes a thirty-second conversation with a doctor can leave a person feeling like his whole world has caved in.

For some, the crisis struck at work. Your best employee, or your partner, or your key account executive announces that he is quitting and he is going to work with your biggest competitor. A firm that owes you a lot of money announces bankruptcy and you realize it could be devastating for you. Your boss unexpectedly hands over your final check, terminates your employment, and someone watches as you pack your things and then escorts you to the door. In two minutes it feels like your whole world has caved in.

Crisis comes in so many different shapes, forms, and wrappings:

"Mom, Dad, I'm so sorry. I'm pregnant."

"Phil, this is hard for me to say. I'm moving out and I'm taking the kids."

"Sue, I can't keep it a secret anymore. I've been having an affair for two years."

"Mr. and Mrs. Davis, your son is down here at headquarters on a drug possession charge."

The Evil One's options seem to be infinite. Sometimes Satan does his work slowly and subtly ... dart by dart, scheme by scheme, he tries to wear us down. At other times, he seems to organize all the forces of hell for an all-out frontal attack designed to crush our faith. Satan's objective is to convince a follower of Jesus that the whole world has caved in. Hope is gone. Life is over. And nothing will ever be the same again.

Making the Connection

1. Describe a time when things came crashing down in your life or in the life of someone you care about.

Knowing and Being Known

Read Psalm 46

2. How could this psalm offer comfort and hope to a person who feels the bottom of their life has just fallen out?

God is there for us, to help, give strength to cope.

3. What do you learn about the character and power of God in this psalm?

all powerful
nothing is too much
loving and caring
makes wars cease
ever present
fortress/refuge

What is God doing when we are in a time of crisis?

testing
comforting
protecting
being there

God Is Our Safe Harbor

When I was in junior high my father and I were out on his sailboat on Lake Michigan. About an hour out from South Haven, Michigan, on the east side of the lake, my dad said, "What do you say we sail all night over to Chicago, one hundred miles, just you and me?" I thought that would be a great adventure. So, off we sailed.

Halfway across Lake Michigan, in the middle of the night, we were hit by a fierce storm. Raging winds howled and waves were breaking all over the boat. I knew we were in trouble when my father tied me to the boat with a very heavy rope and said, "Don't go anywhere." Then he went up on the foredeck to make some sail adjustments while I stayed leashed to the helm.

We fought that storm all night and toward the morning hours we could finally see the lights of Chicago in the distance. We just kept struggling and sailing and crashing through the waves until we passed through the breakwater into the harbor. As we tied up to the dock, for the first time in my young life, I had a vivid understanding and appreciation of how wonderful a protected harbor can be. Just three hundred yards away from where we sat, Lake Michigan was still churning and dangerous. But we had found a shelter, a hiding place from the storm.

Read Psalm 46:1, 7, 11 and Psalm 107:23 – 32

4. God is called a refuge, a fortress, and a harbor. How have you experienced God as a <u>safe haven</u> and a place of protection in the middle of life's storms?

5. One of the ways God will often create a harbor for us is by surrounding us with a wall of people who love us, encourage us, and pray for us. If you are in a stormy time of life, how could your group members surround you and function as a storm wall?

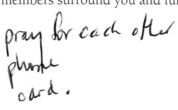
pray for each other
phone
card.

God Is Our Strength

In Psalm 46:1 we are told that God is more than just a refuge. He is also our strength. To continue with the harbor metaphor, it seems that what the psalmist is driving at is that we can't stay in the harbor forever. We can't hide in a refuge permanently. Sooner or later we must get back to the rigors of everyday life. No matter what we have faced, there comes a time when we need to press on. As peaceful and safe as a refuge feels, God calls us to receive his strength so we can continue on with life.

Sooner or later we have to go back to work, even if it means going back with trembling knees. Eventually we have to start relating to the family again. After time in the harbor, we have to pick up our mantle of responsibility in the church. With time we have to face all of the other tasks that await us in life. God knows that we need a source of strength beyond ourselves. So he promises his strength for us to press on.

Read Psalm 46:1 – 3 and Isaiah 40:28 – 31

6. Describe a time that God gave you strength and courage to press on even when you felt you did not have what it would take in your own power.

7. Choose *one* of the statements below and tell your group what counsel you would give to a person who makes that statement:

    • "I will not press on and step out until I can be sure that the storm is gone and it won't come back!"

    • "I would like to think I could move forward after what I have faced, but I just don't have the strength!"

    • "I know that God promises strength for the weary, but he has no idea what I am facing here!"

8. In the same way that God offers refuge through other people, he also offers strength. Three or four people can lift a bigger load than one person. If you need strength to press on in your life, how might your group members help lift some of the load with you?

prayer
listening
sharing.

God Is Our Present Help

As we walk through this life we should not live with a constant feeling that tragedy is on the horizon. Instead, we should be consumed by a profound awareness that God is near, ever-present, and ready to help us through each day.

There are many ways we can open spiritual connections that will allow us to sense God's ever-present care in richer and more personal ways. We can develop disciplines of solitude, silence, and prayer. Each of these nurtures a meaningful, two-way conversation with our God, who is near. We can read Scripture and meditate on biblical truths, letting the Word of God bring assurance and affirmation of the Spirit's presence with us. We can connect with other Christians and share sweet moments of fellowship, sing songs of praise, and offer acts of service to the broken and hurting in the name of Jesus. All of these create a climate where experiencing God as our present help is natural.

God is near ... closer than we think.

Read Psalm 46

9. List some of the images in Psalm 46 that paint a picture of hope and assurance that God is always with us.

10. What gets in the way of your experiencing God's presence through the course of an ordinary day?

What disciplines and habits have you discovered that help you connect with God and experience his presence throughout the day?

11. As you listened to other group members talk about what helps them experience God's presence through an ordinary day, what was one idea that really struck you?

How might you incorporate this discipline into your life?

Celebrating and Being Celebrated

For centuries believers who thought their worlds were caving in around them have drawn near to God in their moments of need. In their fear and brokenness, with tears and anxiety, they have poured out their hearts to the Lord and have found that God was a refuge, a shelter, a hiding place. In the middle of those storms, God was more real than ever before.

Take time as a group to pray together, offering up prayers of thanks, praise, and celebration for how God has been a safe harbor in the middle of life's storms.

Loving and Being Loved

When we have gone through storms in life, God has sent other people to fortify us and offer the strong support of God's family. These people have revealed the presence and love of God to us in our most difficult times. Think about a person God has used this way in your life and let them know what a difference they made. Thank them for being a conduit of God's presence, strength, and love.

Serving and Being Served

Make a list of two or three people you know who are currently experiencing life's storms. Commit to pray for them over the next month. Use some of the ideas below to give direction and shape to your prayers:

> God, be their safe harbor and refuge as they go through this storm.
>
> Spirit of God, reveal your presence in the midst of their storm that they might know you are an ever-present help in their time of need.
>
> Jesus, grant strength for this person to make it through, even when they can't see the harbor from where they are.
>
> Lord, bring people around this friend so they might feel the strong support and fellowship of other Christ followers.

The God of Delight

PSALM 37

Some Bible verses have been abused and misused over the years. They're like blood in the water for sharks ... things can turn into a feeding frenzy and get very dangerous. This is exactly what seems to happen when people wrench Psalm 37:4 out of context ... they can go wild with it.

> Delight yourself in the LORD
>   and he will give you the desires of your heart.

You can read this verse and easily imagine where people might wander. Some say it means that if you become a Christ follower, God will give you everything you could ever want. Others say that if you live a good Christian life and exercise your faith confidently, all you have to do is tell God what you want, and it is yours. There are quite a few people who take this verse (and a few others) and interpret it to say that God is obligated to do whatever we say.

Most days you could turn on the TV or radio and find someone preaching a message that gives the impression that God, the maker of heaven and earth, exists to fulfill our every wish and do our bidding at all times. They confidently declare, "Trust God and you will be healthy, wealthy, happy, thin, and your skin will clear up!" That might sound overstated, but this kind of message is being preached by people who take Psalm 37:4 and stretch it as far as they can.

This verse, and others like it, have been so widely abused that some Christians discount it all together. They steer clear of this verse and the topic of God giving us the desires of our heart because they don't want to abuse it. In many cases, this beautiful promise and wonderful expression of God's character has been relegated to the inactive file.

1. How have you seen people abuse Bible passages in an attempt to build a religious system that fits their needs, promises what they want, or gives them control over God?

   John 5:14-15

   What are some of the dangers of this kind of misuse of the Bible?

   *we are constantly grasping and changing
   our desires are never perfect*

   Why is it important that we not relegate these passages to an "inactive file" just because some people abuse them?

Knowing and Being Known

Read Psalm 37

2. Psalm 37 paints a vivid contrast between those who follow God and those who rebel against him. As you read through the psalm, gather information on these two groups of people and record what you learn in the boxes on page 42:

What I learn about those who follow God:

Verse from Psalm 37	What I learn about those who follow God (those who trust him, delight in him, commit their way to him, are still before him)
	they will inherit the land
	bless us, help us

What I learn about those who rebel against God:

Verse from Psalm 37	What I learn about those who rebel against God (those who are "wicked," "evil," and "enemies" of God)
	cut off
	swords will pierce
	perish

3. What are some of the clear and vivid contrasts between these two groups of people?

land
offspring
salvation / perish
food / famine

42

How do you see these same contrasts functioning in our world today?

suffering as a result of wicked.

The Depraved Desires of Humanity

We are people overflowing with desires. Little children express with bold clarity, "I want food, candy, toys, my way, and so much more." Teenagers continue the chant, "I want new clothes, a nice computer, an upgrade for my cell phone, more freedom, a car (and a gas card if you don't mind), and, and, and ..." When we grow up and become adults we mature and the endless litany of "I want" comes to an end, right? Wrong! We simply adjust our list: "I want a raise, a new car, more acknowledgments, a bigger house." These desires seem to grow with time rather than decrease with time.

We can chuckle at children or teenagers who demand more and more. We can excuse ourselves or rationalize the bottomless pit of our desires by saying, "We're only human." But our endless desire for more is a serious problem. Theologians have identified this condition as depravity. We are all born with a sinful orientation; only following Jesus can keep us from trying to fulfill our destructive desires and shipwrecking our lives.

Read Psalm 37:1 – 4, 12 – 14, 20 – 21, 32

4. What are some of the signs we can see, just by a casual look around us, that the pursuit of sinful, depraved desires is causing pain and brokenness in our world?

depraved – marked by corruption or evil

deprived – marked by deprivation esp. of the necessities of life or of healthful env. influences

43

5. When we become followers of Jesus, our desires begin to change. Not always overnight, but bit by bit the Holy Spirit changes us from the inside out. What is an example of a desire in you that has changed as you have grown in maturity as a follower of Christ?

Delight in the Lord

What does it means to "Delight yourself in the Lord"? It is much deeper than walking down an aisle to make a first-time commitment to Jesus, as important as that is. It is more substantial than attending a local church, though I strongly encourage you to do that. It goes beyond saying daily prayers, reading the Bible, seeking to be obedient, or serving in the church, as valuable as all of these are.

To delight yourself in the Lord is to throw your whole self into the arms of the God who loves you beyond description. It means finding your most valuable treasure in your relationship with Jesus. It's about rejoicing in who he is, loving him with all your heart, soul, mind, and strength.

This delight happens when we discover our desperate need for a Savior; grows as we glimpse his character; goes deeper as we experience his amazing grace, walk in his incomparable power, and see his glorious face. This delight grows day by day as we walk in the presence of our loving God.

Read Psalm 37:1 – 7, 18 – 19, 23 – 31, 37 – 40

6. According to this psalm, what are some of the reasons we should take delight in the Lord?

future for man of peace   *give you desires of heart*   *dwell in the land*

your righteousness shine like the dawn   *prote*

delivers them   *justice of your cause like the noon day sun*   *feet will not sl*

safe pasture   *inheritance will endure forever*   *enjoy plenty*   *the Lord upholds him*

44

7. Share about a time in your life when you realized that you were growing in the delight of the Lord and you could see your love and passion for him moving you to new places of devotion.

8. What are some of the life choices, disciplines, or habits that help us grow in the delight of the Lord?

   know God's character and personality, identity
   God's power active, faithfulness
   God's friendship and fellowship

The Desires of Your Heart

When we discover a relationship with God through Christ, and when we begin to delight in the Lord, one of the first transformations we experience is that the Holy Spirit starts changing our old desires. Second Corinthians 5:17 says, "Therefore, if anyone is in Christ, he is a new creation; the old has gone, the new has come!" Our old desires start to pass away—not all at once, but gradually, slowly, and systematically. We find ourselves falling out of love with things we used to obsess over. The taste for certain things starts to wear off. Day by day, year by year, the Holy Spirit transforms our lives.

Then, in a mysterious way, we begin to long for new things. Our desires and tastes change. Where we used to spend a Thursday afternoon yearning for Friday night at the bar, we find ourselves looking forward to gathering with God's family for worship on the weekend. Where we used to plan and scheme about how we could earn more money to buy the next big toy, we find our desire is to leverage our money to help those in need and feed the poor. Instead of desiring power and influence over others, we begin noticing ways we can serve and lift people up. As our desires become more and more reflective of the heart of God, we are ready to receive the desires of our heart.

Read Psalm 37:4

9. Discuss this statement: *Sometimes the best, safest, and wisest thing God could do is not give us the desires of our heart.*

10. As time passes and we mature in our faith, our desires change to look more and more like the desires of Jesus. Name one specific desire of yours that you would like to see changed in this way.

How can your group members pray for you as you seek the Holy Spirit's power to see this area of desire transformed?

Celebrating and Being Celebrated

In this session we have looked at delighting in the Lord in primarily a personal way. Now, as a group, take turns sharing things about God that bring delight to your life. You can use the images in Psalm 37, other passages from the Bible, or stories from your own walk with Jesus and life experience.

Loving and Being Loved

As you have meditated on Psalm 37, the Holy Spirit may have convicted you of an area of desire in your life that is still far from what God wants. Take time on your own to confess this area to God … he already knows all about it. Ask for the Holy Spirit's strength and his consistent reminders of how he wants to change this desire. Give God a gift of your love, a willingness to have this desire changed to reflect what honors Jesus.

Serving and Being Served

If you have an area of desire you have been feeding, but you know it is not God's will for you, invite a group member or a trusted Christian friend to serve you. Share your area of struggle with someone who will:

- Keep it in confidence,
- Pray for you faithfully,
- Check in with you weekly and ask how you are doing in your efforts to surrender this area of struggle to God.

The Wonder of God

PSALM 139

Sometimes David begins a psalm with an exclamation like, "Bless the Lord," or "Praise the Lord," or "Thanks to God!" Psalm 139 feels very different: No less passionate than other psalms, there is a sober, awe-inspired quietness about it. David begins, "O LORD, you have searched me and you know me ..."

I picture David with his head bowed down, his heart lifted up, a mere whisper on his lips. He admits, right from the start, that words can't possibly convey the wonder and majesty of God. David, the poet laureate, is left with quill and blank parchment because he is attempting to describe that which is too wonderful for words. He simply groans with feelings of utter inadequacy. Then with uncharacteristic directness and no further flowery imagery, David acknowledges and declares that God is omniscient (all-knowing), omnipresent (present everywhere), and omnipotent (all-powerful). By the end of the psalm King David—ruler, warrior, man of wealth, top gun—humbly submits himself to the reality that God is more wonderful than he can imagine or explain.

David is in good company. All through the Bible we encounter people who expressed amazement at the wonder of God. Isaiah caught just a brief glimpse of the glory of God in a vision and cried out, "Woe to me!... I am ruined! For I am a man of unclean lips, and I live among a people of unclean lips, and my eyes have seen the King, the LORD Almighty" (Isaiah 6:5). Job, after a period of intense suffering and extended debates with his friends, declares to God, "My ears had heard of you but now my eyes have seen you. Therefore I despise myself and repent in dust and ashes" (Job 42:5–6). The apostle Peter witnessed a miracle of Jesus, fell on his knees, and gasped, "Go away from me, Lord; I am a sinful man!" (Luke 5:8).

Making the Connection

1. Describe a time you got a glimpse of God's wonder. How did you feel and respond?

Knowing and Being Known

Read Psalm 139:1 – 18

2. Theologians have tried to develop language to explain the wonder of God. In a sense, they are using words to describe the indescribable! But, as we seek to know and follow God, these words can be a helpful tool. Look at each of the theological terms below and on page 50, and seek to identify how God reveals himself as omniscient, omnipresent, and omnipotent.

   • **God is omniscient**: This means that God knows all things, that nothing is outside of his ever-watching gaze. What are some of the statements or truths declared by David in this psalm that reveal God's omniscience?

   • **God is omnipresent**: This means that God is everywhere at the same time, unlimited by time, space, or place. What are some of the statements or truths declared by David in this psalm that reveal God's omnipresence?

- **God is omnipotent**: This means that God is all-powerful; nothing is too difficult for him. What are some of the statements or truths declared by David in this psalm that reveal God's omnipotence?

3. Psalm 139 paints a vivid, personal picture of a God who knows all, sees all, who is everywhere, and who can do anything. How might *one* of the following kinds of people respond to the vision of God presented in this psalm?

- A follower of Christ who is seeking to walk close with God and serve him faithfully

- A follower of Christ who is resisting God's leading and living in consistent disobedience

- A person who is spiritually seeking and wants to know if there really is a God out there

- A person who defines God as some kind of "life force" that got the universe started, but who has no interest or involvement in our lives today

Our Omniscient God

God knows all the vast secrets of the universe—the intricate mysteries of the atom, the complex workings of all life forms—but this is not what captures David's heart. What causes David to stop in dumbfounded wonder is that God knows *him!* Every little detail of David's day takes place under the watchful and loving eyes of God. Each time David sits down or stands up, God notices. Every deed, every activity, every movement ... nothing he does escapes God's notice. It is like God has a divine GPS and David is always on the center of the screen. God has a copy of David's itinerary before it is planned or printed.

David also ponders the wonder of God's knowing not only what David is doing, but what he is thinking. Every passing thought, every midnight musing, every calculating strategy, every private worship time, pleasing or not—none is secret to the omniscient God.

Read Psalm 139:1 – 6

4. David had this moment of clarity and awareness: *God knows everything about me. He knows where I am, what I think, and even the words I want to say, but have the wisdom to bite my tongue. God knows it all!* Tell about a moment in your life when you were struck by the awareness that God knows everything about you.

How did this make you feel?

5. If you were to live each day with a profound awareness of the omniscience of God, how might this influence *one* of the following things?

- Where you go
- What you say
- How you serve those in need
- What you daydream about
- How you speak *to* others
- How you speak *of* others
- How you use your resources
- What you watch on TV, at the movies, or on your computer

6. What can we do to raise our own personal awareness, in the course of a normal day, that God is omniscient?

Our Omnipresent God

Again, David gets very personal. He ponders if there is any place in all of creation where God would not be present, holding David's hand. That's the picture. It is very intimate. David is aware that even if he could fly to the other side of the sea, God would still be there ... holding his hand.

Many years ago my wife, Lynne, and I took our two kids to Disney World. As we stood in line for the haunted house attraction, I said to my then-six-year-old son, "Do you want me to hold your hand while we go in here?" "No," he confidently declared. But I left my hands out of my pockets and in plain sight of the kids. Three steps into the attraction, as you could probably guess, there were two little hands in mine holding on like a vise. I didn't withdraw my hands. Good fathers and good mothers don't ever remove their hands.

David declared what we all learn over time: our heavenly Father doesn't ever withdraw his hand from his children. Wherever we go, wherever we run, wherever we try to hide, God's hand is right there. What a beautiful and powerful picture of the omnipresence of God!

Read Psalm 139:7 – 12

7. Tell about a time of loss, sorrow, or pain when an outside observer might have concluded that God was far from you, but you felt his loving hand holding you close. How did God reveal his presence with you during that time?

8. The intimate picture of God's presence as a divine hand holding our hand is clear in this psalm (v. 10). How might such an awareness of God's omnipresence bring comfort to:

   • A child who is afraid of the dark (see vv. 11 – 12)

   • An adult going through a difficult time in a relationship

   • A family facing financial struggles

- A couple facing marriage tensions

- A single person who hopes to marry some day

- A college student away from home for the first time

Our Omnipotent God

Though David could have used countless other examples of God's omnipotence, he is caught up in how personal God is, and what could be more intimate than forming a child in the womb of a mother?

David worships God for having the power necessary to author, engineer, and energize individual human lives. Hurling the stars into space is amazing, stacking up the mountains is remarkable, filling the ocean beds is beyond comprehension, but designing and forming a human life, that is an absolutely, positively overwhelming feat accomplished only by an omnipotent God whose wonder is beyond description.

Read Psalm 139:13 – 18

9. Often, when we think of the limitless power of God, we focus on the vastness of the universe, the heights of the mountains, or the depths of the seas. Instead of looking at the very large in God's creation, consider the very small. If you have ever seen an ultrasound picture of a baby in the womb, or felt a baby kick, how did this moment reveal the wonderful power of God?

10. Take a moment to read Psalm 139:13–18 aloud and in unison as a group. Read it as a declaration of what God has done and who you are. (If you don't all have a Bible or the same translation, this passage is printed in the Leader's Notes for this session on pages 79–80.) If you take this passage seriously, what does it say about you?

What does it say about how God feels about you?

Celebrating and Being Celebrated

Take time in prayer to celebrate who God is and what that means for those who follow him. Use the structure of this psalm to guide your prayers:

- Praise God for his omniscience and awareness of all you think, say, or do. Then, ask for power to live in a way that pleases him as he watches your life.
- Thank God for being a Father who is omnipresent, who holds your hand and never lets go. Pray for an awareness of his presence and strength to follow his daily leading.
- Celebrate God's omnipotent power in creation, including his intimate formation of your life. Pray for faith in God's power to lead and direct you each and every day.

Loving and Being Loved

After proclaiming God's omniscience, omnipresence, and omnipotence, David is staggered that anyone could still disbelieve and hate God. So, in verses 19–22 of this psalm he expresses anger and hatred toward such people. But suddenly it seems to strike David that perhaps there is an inner room of defiance, a secret storehouse of disobedience in his own life. The thought terrifies him. Thus he ends the psalm where he begins . . . with an awareness that God needs to search our hearts. He prays:

> Search me, O God, and know my heart;
>> test me and know my anxious thoughts.
> See if there is any offensive way in me,
>> and lead me in the way everlasting. (vv. 23–24)

Take time in the coming week to get alone with God and this passage. Pray through it. Ask God to search, test, and redirect you in any area of disobedience and rebellion.

Serving and Being Served

In this psalm we are reminded that God has a plan for our lives (v. 16). He has put us on this earth for a purpose. And he gives us power to fulfill his purposes for us. Take time before God in the coming week to evaluate your commitment to serve him and others. You have been given a spiritual gift from God. In his omnipotent power, he can give you all you need to exercise this gift for his glory and to strengthen his church. If you are not serving in some capacity in your church or community, consider taking a step and investigating how you can become involved.

Worthy of Worship

PSALM 100

God is worthy of worship … all the time. What changes in the worship equation is never God, but us. At times we are deeply committed in faith and ready to give praise freely and passionately. At other times we become casual or comfortable in our faith and forget to give God the worship he deserves.

Casual Christians claim they have made a commitment to Jesus. They call themselves Christ followers but that is about the only outer sign of their inner change. A casual observer could never tell they are Christians by their conversations, value systems, personal schedule, relationships, or priorities. Quite frankly, their lives do not look all that different from people who are not believers in Jesus. When it comes to worship, this does not show up on their radar as a priority or value. Simply put, the only indication these people are Christians is their claim to be one.

Comfortable Christians have a mild case of Christianity. They profess faith in Jesus like the casual Christian, but they also pray, attend some church services, find a comfortable level of fellowship, choose safe amounts of money to give, and adopt an easy lifestyle pattern. They are too concerned about being comfortable to follow the leading of the Holy Spirit, take bold steps of faith, or reach out beyond themselves. They show up for church services, but their view of worship is more self-centered. Their driving concern is *what do I like, what do I get out of the experience, and how does worship "bless" me?*

Committed Christians have a severe case of Christianity. They are driven, even dangerous offensive weapons for Christ. These bold followers tell God, "I want you to take my life and use me for your glory." Their Christianity is apparent to everyone who meets them … it shines through. These people see the world through the lens of the Holy Spirit and everything is impacted by the presence of God. Their joy quotient is high. When it comes to worship, they are reckless, passionate, and surrendered. They have a vision of God that compels them to shout, sing, give thanks, and celebrate God's presence in a way that is contagious and authentic.

Psalm 100 paints a picture of a Committed Christian, a person who has opened his or her eyes to see the majesty, power, and worth of God. And, in response, this person responds with words, actions, and a life that declares, "God is worthy of worship, all the time!"

Making the Connection

1. We all have seasons when we function as a Casual Christian, a Comfortable Christian, and a Committed Christian. As you consider the following four areas, write down a few brief thoughts about what your life looks like when you are functioning in each of these modes:

Area of my life: My time alone with Jesus for fellowship with him and spiritual growth.

- When I am a ... Casual Christian

- When I am a ... Comfortable Christian

- When I am a ... Committed Christian

Area of my life: My participation in worship among God's people at church services.

- When I am a ... Casual Christian

- When I am a ... Comfortable Christian

- When I am a ... Committed Christian

Area of my life: My service and the ministry I offer to people in and out of the church.

- When I am a ... Casual Christian

- When I am a ... Comfortable Christian

- When I am a ... Committed Christian

Area of my life: Some other area of my life and faith:

_____

- When I am a ... Casual Christian

- When I am a ... Comfortable Christian

- When I am a ... Committed Christian

Share about one area and how your life changes depending on what kind of "Christian" life you are leading.

Read Psalm 100

2. What are the qualities and characteristics of God mentioned in this psalm that could lead you to a place of worship and praise?

Take a moment as a group to pray, praising God for how these qualities have been experienced in your lives.

3. The psalmist has a vision of God that leads to passionate and active worship. What are some of the expressions of worship captured in this psalm, and how can these shape the way we worship God?

Read Psalm 100:1 – 2; Daniel 6:6 – 10; and Acts 16:22 – 25

4. Circumstances change, problems come and go, but God is the same yesterday, today, and forever. Share about a time when you faced the reality of heartache or pain yet found yourself worshiping and praising God in the midst of life's uncertainties.

A Praiseworthy God

People who are truly committed to God are overwhelmed by the simple reality that he is worthy of praise. The apostle Paul was beat up and tossed into prison, but he kept on singing. Daniel was warned, under penalty of death, to stop praying to God, but he could not help himself; three times a day he got on his knees to lift up prayers and thanksgiving to God. When Job was sitting on a heap of ashes, enduring physical and emotional turmoil, he still offered heartfelt prayers and praise to God. This theme of unstoppable worship runs all through the Bible and the history of the church. Consider these words spoken by Genesius of Rome before he was martyred under the emperor Diocletian in 285 AD.

> There is but one king that I know;
> It is he that I love and worship.
> If I were to be killed a thousand times
> for my loyalty to him,
> I would still be his servant.
> Christ is on my lips,
> Christ is in my heart;
> No amount of suffering will take him from me.

5. Psalm 100:1–2 includes the words "joy," "gladness," and "joyful." If someone were to visit your church and look at the faces of worshipers, listen to the songs, and pick up the feelings of those gathered, how do you think they would describe the atmosphere of the group?

What can we do to bring more joy and gladness to our worship experiences?

A God Who Is God Alone

There is only one God. He has revealed himself as Father, Son, and Holy Spirit. We live in a pluralistic world that wants us to embrace and affirm all religious systems as equally true and valid. The problem is, the Bible does not teach or allow this. As a matter of fact, in Old Testament times, there were many religions and all kinds of worship options. Into this highly eclectic religious atmosphere the psalmist declares, "Know that the Lord is God." And in Deuteronomy, we read, "Hear, O Israel: The Lord our God, the Lord is one" (6:4). Later, in Jesus' day, as the world continued to spin out new religions, Jesus was clear that there is only one God, and faith in him alone is what we need for salvation. He said, "I am the way and the truth and the life. No one comes to the Father except through me" (John 14:6).

Read Psalm 100:3; Deuteronomy 4:35 – 40; and Exodus 20:1 – 6

6. What are some of the ways the world is trying to press followers of Jesus to embrace and accept other religious systems as valid?

Why is it important that we hold to the biblical truth that there is one God who is revealed in the Bible?

7. Knowing who God is and what he has done shapes our worship. Choose *one* of the statements below (drawn from Psalm 100:3) and tell about how this reality might impact the way we worship:

- Reality … there is only one God, the Lord
- Reality … he is the Creator and we are his creation
- Reality … he is the Shepherd and we are his sheep

A God Deserving Thanksgiving Offerings

When we read "thanksgiving" in Psalm 100:4 we naturally think about words of thanks. But the psalm's first readers would have thought immediately of the "thank offering," a gift of their material goods that was offered up with a joyful and thankful heart. The picture here reminds us that part of our worship is bringing material gifts that we can offer up to God. When we see God as worthy of worship and when we are Committed Christians, giving from our storehouse of resources is no longer a chore, but a privilege.

Read Psalm 100:4 and 2 Corinthians 9:6 – 8

8. Along with songs of praise and words of thanks, we are invited to bring offerings to God as part of our worship. How is the giving of tithes and offerings an act of worship?

9. What are some things that can get in the way of our being generous toward God and giving offerings freely and joyfully?

What helps you come to a place of joyfully and generously giving offerings to God?

A God Who Is Good

We use the word "good" to describe all kinds of people and things. A man says, "I have a good wife." A woman declares, "I have a good husband." People say, "We have a good church." We tell friends, "I found a good restaurant." So when the psalmist says, "The Lord is good," we might not grasp the full impact of the words. Saying that God is good means something entirely different than parents saying they have good kids. God does not act good just once in awhile ... he *is* good, intrinsically good, good by nature. God can't be anything but good. And he will never run out of goodness from today through eternity. Now *that* is a God worthy of worship!

Read Psalm 100:5

10. Finish *one* of the statements below:

    • I experienced God's goodness in my life when he ...
    • I came to understand God's enduring love for me when ...
    • I know God's faithfulness continues from generation to generation because he has ...

11. As you look at the church you are part of (it could be a new church plant or a congregation celebrating decades of ministry), how has God shown his enduring love and faithfulness to this body of Christ followers?

Celebrating and Being Celebrated

People in every church use their gifts to help the congregation grow as worshipers. They might play instruments, sing, preach, lead in prayer, or use technical gifts to run a sound system or develop videos. Whether up front or behind the scenes, these people find real joy in helping others come into God's presence.

In the coming week affirm and thank at least one person who helps make your church services possible. Thank God for these people and let them know that you celebrate the way they use their gifts to glorify God and touch the lives of people in the church.

Loving and Being Loved

Spend several minutes as a group praying to the One who is worthy of worship, using Psalm 100 to direct your prayer time. Have a group member volunteer to read verse 1, and then lift up prayers in response to this verse. After a few prayers have been offered, read verse 2 and offer prayers in response to its themes. Continue through verse 5, then close in prayer.

Serving and Being Served

When we have our eyes opened and see God as he is, worthy of praise and worship, it is hard to be a Casual Christian or a Comfortable Christian. Recognizing that the Lord is God, our Maker, and our Shepherd compels us to live as a fully Committed Christian, moved to offer our whole life to God. This is our greatest act of worship.

> Therefore, I urge you, brothers, in view of God's mercy, to offer your bodies as living sacrifices, holy and pleasing to God—this is your spiritual act of worship. Do not conform any longer to the pattern of this world, but

be transformed by the renewing of your mind. Then you will be able to test and approve what God's will is—his good, pleasing and perfect will. (Romans 12:1–2)

Offer your life to God as a passionate worshiper, humble servant, and obedient child. Consider using the prayer below in this process of giving yourself fully to God as a Committed Christian.

You are my God! You have given everything for me. You are my Creator and Shepherd. You are my Savior. I don't want to live as a Casual Christian. I will no longer be content getting by as a Comfortable Christian. I want to be a radically Committed Christian. Your Word tells me that when a grain of wheat falls to the ground and dies, it comes back and blossoms. But that doesn't happen until it dies. Jesus, I take a fresh step of faith. I give my life to you in total surrender. I take up your cross to follow you. Let this day, this moment be the beginning of a new chapter in my life of faith. I pray this in the name of my Good Shepherd, Jesus. Amen!

Session One – God Is…
PSALM 103

Questions 2–3

One beautiful thing about Psalm 103 is that it calls us to "forget not all his benefits" and then it goes on to help us remember. In this psalm we find one of the most extensive lists of God's benefits and attributes in the entire Bible. Due to the limitation of space, we will cover only four in the actual session. However, to help you study some of the other attributes mentioned in this psalm, here are a few notes to spark your conversations.

David says our *God is a healing God.* Bound up in the very nature of who God is is a desire for all people to be whole physically as well as spiritually. How do we know this is true? It is easy to come to this conclusion from Scripture. How did God originally create Adam and Eve? They were physically perfect. How does God promise we are going to be in heaven someday when we are in his presence? He says we are going to receive new bodies. There will be no sickness, no sorrow; no pain, illness, or tears. What God intended in the beginning and what God will establish in eternity are indications of his healing heart. We can also know God's heart from the ministry of Jesus, who went from place to place not only saving souls but healing bodies. People didn't have to plead for Jesus to heal them; it's part of his nature. In fact, many times he went out and said, "What would you like me to do for you?" We read that from early morning to late night he would heal people as the needs arose. We have a healing God.

David also says our *God is a satisfying God.* "He satisfies our desires with good things, so that our youth is renewed like the eagle's." As a part of God's nature he desires that, once his people are redeemed and forgiven, they lead satisfied, full, abundant lives. John 10:10 says, "The thief comes only to steal and kill and destroy; I have come that they may have life, and have it to the full."

One more attribute highlighted in this psalm is that our *God is a righteous God.* Throughout history, God was, still is, and always will be righteous. Our God has never made a bad decision or an unfair judgment, nor will he ever in the future. He has never caved in to an outside evil force. We never need lose sleep wondering whether or not God is going to honor our obedience or treat us fairly; he will.

This psalm could give birth to a whole small group study of its own, there is so much more packed into it. If the picture painted by the psalmist in this chapter could be painted on the walls of our hearts, we would follow God with greater passion, serve him with more vigor, and praise him with greater enthusiasm.

Questions 4–5

God wants us to know that forgiveness flows freely from his heart. Eager to pardon, he looks for small indications of true repentance in the lives of broken, sinful people and rushes in to extend amazing grace. Like the father with the prodigal son, as soon as we begin heading home, God is ready to run to us, embrace us, and welcome us home.

He wants to totally remove all sin from our past so that we can feel freed to move on with our lives. David would say to every follower of Christ, "Don't ever underestimate God's pardoning nature, thinking that you have to maneuver or manipulate a pardon out of the heart of an unforgiving God." That is not who God is. He is a pardoning God.

Questions 6–8

God is loving... head-over-heels loving, lay-down-his-life loving, beyond-our-capacity-to-comprehend loving. As the apostle John says, "For God so loved the world that he gave ..." (John 3:16). To know God is to know a perfect, unstoppable love.

We serve an immutable God. "Immutable" is the theologians' word for never-changing. In a world filled with ceaseless transitions, we can be sure that God is the same today as he was yesterday. And tomorrow he will be the same again. What a comforting truth!

We serve a God whose love, justice, righteousness, forgiveness, and other character qualities are not subject to change. His character needs no improvement. Malachi 3:6 says, "I the LORD do not change."

Session Two — Only God
PSALM 62

Question 1

A "God and" person wants his cake and wants to eat it too. He wants what God wants, but he wants what he wants also. He fudges and hedges and juggles and rationalizes in order to perpetuate his chameleon-like charade.

What complicates the matter is that a "God and" person isn't obedient enough to be greatly used by God, which is the thrill of the Christian life. At the same time, he isn't wicked enough to throw caution to the wind and join in the dance with demons and thoroughly waste himself in the folly of sin. People who live this way are caught in the middle. No heavenly thrills, no hellish thrills. This person sort of tortures himself or herself in no man's land.

In Revelation 3:14–22, God himself warns against this kind of life.

Questions 2–3

When we live as "God and" people, we consign ourselves to learning life's lessons the hard way. A love for the praise of others, the things of this world, doing life our own way sends us down all sorts of painful roads.

We have all heard the stories of those who have journeyed this painful road. A person who has lived in the depths of alcoholism might passionately say, "I want to warn others: don't take your first drink, no matter how much you want your friends to accept you." Someone who has been captive to drug addiction might beg others, "Don't take that first pill, smoke that first joint, or experiment with that drug." A Christian man or woman who has lived with the complexities and heartbreak of being married to a nonbeliever might plead, "Never marry an unbeliever." Those who have been buried in debt might say, "Don't get careless with credit cards. They promise freedom but bring bondage." A woman who has battled with emotional anguish and deep loss might say, "Don't get that abortion. Some will tell you it is a quick fix and an easy option. But, slow down; pray; look at other possibilities." This list could go on and on.

When we realize we have made mistakes driven by a "God and" approach to life, God can use us to counsel others. Our experiences can serve as cautions to avoid the same harmful choices.

Questions 4–6

God has made us to live in community. What others think matters to us, and it should ... to an extent. Children should care what their parents think. Friends should respect each other's opinions. Spouses should care about each other's perspectives.

The problem is when the praise of people and the desire to please them drives our lives. Hearing God say, "Well done, good and faithful servant!" (Matthew 25:23) should matter far more than what friends or family think or say about us. When that is the greatest desire of our hearts, then we will not be controlled and misdirected by the need to hear people say, "Great job!"

There is nothing wrong with receiving others' affirmation and encouragement. But when their praise means more than God's praise, we are living a "God and" life and danger is ahead.

Questions 7–9

Jesus was very clear that we cannot love both God and the stuff of this world (Matthew 6:24). This is one of the reasons Scripture calls us to give so often. When we give away money and things, their grip on our hearts is loosened.

Most of us will face the temptation to be "God and" people when it comes to money for our entire lives. That's why we must be aware of the ongoing struggle and commit to fight the battle. Some of our weapons are thankfulness, contentment, tithing, generous giving, and a proper perspective ... remembering that all we have is a gift from God!

Questions 10–11

There come moments in life when we are aware and ready to renounce some tantalizing pleasures of this world, when we realize it is time to burn some bridges that should have been burned a long time ago. At these crossroads we need to say, "I want to be a 'God only' man or a 'God only' woman." This group study might lead some to such a point of decision. If it does, make space for conversation, prayer, and commitment to live in a new and devoted way.

Session Three – God in Crisis
PSALM 46

Questions 1–3

Psalm 46 is about God's presence and strength in the midst of calamity. It is about earth-quaking, mountain-shaking, ocean-foaming crisis moments ... the kind all of us will experience some time in our lives.

I never would have dreamed, when I first went into ministry, that I would hear stories about so much heartbreak, loss, and pain. I guess I was naïve or sheltered. As the years have passed and my circle of friends has grown, rarely does a week go by without my hearing of an unbelievable calamity befalling somebody I know and care about. Many of these heartrending times have nothing to do with sin or bad choices. They are just the suffering that seems to come with being a human being who walks on this earth.

The good news of Psalm 46 is *not* that God will protect us from any and all suffering, but that he *will* be our shelter in the midst of the storm. The psalmist calls us to run to God and discover that he is our shelter, refuge, and safe harbor during life's storms. In those moments when we run to the Lord and pour out our hearts to him, his presence becomes real and we discover that he alone understands what we are facing.

In the safe harbor of God's presence, we learn that the Almighty God who placed the planets in their positions is more tender, gentler, and warmer than we ever dreamed. He is the one who can make us feel safe, secure, and protected, no matter what storm rages.

Questions 4–5

Psalm 46 does not concern itself so much with the "why" of tragedy, but more with the "what to do" when tragedy occurs.

The truth is, none of us will be spared from the storms of life; God never promises to insulate his children from every adversity. Those who pretend to speak for God and declare that faithful Christians will never suffer or face turmoil are simply misled and misleading. Yes, God protects us from some painful circumstances, but more importantly he promises to accompany us through them. This is no small promise.

The first line of Psalm 46 assures us that God is our refuge. When it seems like your whole world has caved in, when you are reeling and uncertain, feeling exposed, frightened, and ready to collapse, you have a refuge in God. Worry about other concerns later, and solve your theological problems at another time. In the middle of a storm, the most important priority is finding a shelter. The best way to do that is to run to God.

For those who feel compelled to figure God out and explain all of life's struggles, I suggest a humble reading of Isaiah 55:9:

> As the heavens are higher than the earth,
>   so are my ways higher than your ways
>   and my thoughts than your thoughts.

Some mysteries we will never understand. Certain tragedies that come our way won't make sense until we meet God face-to-face in heaven. When the world caves in, wise people do not spend a lot of time asking why. Instead, they run to God's open arms, trusting, just trusting, that he will be the refuge they so desperately need.

Questions 6–8

The Bible is filled with passages about the strength God offers in our times of weakness. Here are just a few:

> but those who hope in the Lord
>   will renew their strength.

> They will soar on wings like eagles;
>   they will run and not grow weary,
>   they will walk and not be faint. (Isaiah 40:31)

> You, dear children, are from God and have overcome them, because the one who is in you is greater than the one who is in the world. (1 John 4:4)

I can do everything through him who gives me strength. (Philippians 4:13)

That is why, for Christ's sake, I delight in weaknesses, in insults, in hardships, in persecutions, in difficulties. For when I am weak, then I am strong. (2 Corinthians 12:10)

Yet, even with these promises, there are moments our hearts can grow faint. Isaiah speaks of eagle's wings helping us soar, but sometimes we can feel like a lame duck. We know the One who dwells in us is great, but some days we don't feel great. We know God's power is available, but sometimes we are not sure how to appropriate it. In these moments, we learn to hold on, even when our eyes can't see deliverance on the way. We learn to press on with a strength that only God can provide, clinging desperately to our faith even through our tears.

Question 9–11

Even when we experience God as our refuge and our strength, we can still struggle with wondering if he will always be near and ready to help us. You can find yourself living in fear of another calamity, looking over your shoulder waiting for the other shoe to drop. You say to yourself, "Maybe I weathered this one, but I will never be able to endure another major heartache."

What we really need in these moments is a regular reminder of God's presence in our lives and his commitment to help us in our times of need. And that is exactly what Psalm 46 promises. God wants to be our constant companion. When the earth quakes, the mountains begin to tremble, or we see whitecaps on the seas, we need not freeze in terror and expect the worst. Instead, we know that the God who made the heavens and the earth is near, watching over us.

We hear God say, "I am your God. I am bigger than any calamity you are experiencing. I am bigger than any crisis. I am a refuge. I am your strength. I am a present helper. I have it all under control and I love you. So turn to me, trust in me, run to me, and find me to be all you need, even in the storms of your life."

Session Four — The God of Delight
PSALM 37

Question 1

First John 5:14–15 (and verses like it) used to bother me. The passage says: "This is the confidence we have in approaching God: that if we ask anything according to his will, he hears us. And if we know that he hears us—whatever we ask—we know that we have what we asked of him." I would say, "Ah, but there's a catch in there, that little phrase *according to his will*. How do I know what his will is?"

When we delight ourselves in the Lord, he begins a process of purging our old passions and desires. At the same time, he births and initiates new desires. If our hearts and God's heart beat together on these matters, we can be confident that he will give us our requests. But, if we are operating in a place of spiritual immaturity, seeking the same self-centered and hedonistic desires we had before becoming Christ followers, we can't expect God to give us anything we want, ask, or demand.

Questions 2–3

Woven through the fabric of Psalm 37 are three stories. First is the story of God, the giver of true delight. Second is the story of people who follow God and let him change their desires to look like his. These people will receive the desires of their hearts. Third is the story of the "wicked." These are people whose hearts do not beat with the heart of God. Their desires are anti-God and the end of their road is destruction.

Questions 4–5

Theologians talk about depravity as that evil nature or wicked inclination of a person who has not yet been cleansed of their sin through faith in Jesus and changed by the power of the Holy Spirit. It is important that we understand this thing called depravity . . . these evil desires. If we don't, we will miss the message of Psalm 37.

After the fall, we read in Genesis 6:5 that God observed that every thought in the minds and hearts of people was wicked . . . all the time (an observation that resulted in the flood). The

75

prophet Jeremiah noted the same thing when he wrote, "The heart is deceitful above all things and beyond cure. Who can understand it?" (Jeremiah 17:9).

Unchecked and unsanctified desire can lead people down wrong paths. We are not just talking about ancient people. We are not just talking about the criminals who make the headlines on the evening news. We're talking about nice people like you and me. We are all born in sin and are totally depraved. Until God takes hold of our lives and the Spirit begins a process of transformation, our desires will always lead to spiritual death.

Questions 6–8

Some people begin to delight in the Lord when they explore God's identity and discover that his character and personality are wonderful beyond words, even more wonderful than they dreamed. These people recognize just how graciously, tenderly, and kindly he has always treated them. They come to understand that his grace really is sufficient, his wisdom is unsearchable.

Others grow in their delight in the Lord when they see his power active in their lives. Over time they build a faith portfolio, a scrapbook of answered prayers and divine interventions in their lives.

Still others go deeper into the delight of the Lord as they discover God's friendship and fellowship. They know him as a constant companion who will never leave them or forsake them. No matter what helps us grow in our delight of the Lord, when it happens, our desires continue to change. The more we delight in the Lord, the more our desires reflect the heart of Jesus.

Questions 9–10

Even when we come to faith in Christ and the Holy Spirit takes up residence in our hearts, we will face temptation. Our desires are in the process of being changed, but they are never perfect. That is why it is so dangerous when people propagate a theology that says God will always give us what we desire. Sometimes the best thing God can do is tell us, "No!" He alone knows when our desires are right and we are ready to have them fulfilled. Along the way we need to be patient and trust in his wise decisions.

One of the greatest joys of the Christian life is watching God at work in our lives. As we take time to look back and realize that we are being changed and that our desires are starting to reflect his heart ... wow! What joy!

What are some of the new desires God gives us? Try some of these on for size:

- *The desire to be conformed into the image of Christ.* You find yourself praying, "I want to be changed to be more like Jesus, your Son, so break me and mold me and fill me and use me."
- *The desire to be faithful.* You say, "Lord, more than I want to be famous, I want to be faithful. More than I want to be known, I want to know you."
- *The desire to live a surrendered life.* You cry out, "God, more than I want possessions, I want your Holy Spirit to have complete possession of me. I want to offer my life as a living sacrifice. I want every part of my life yielded to you."

Session Five – The Wonder of God
PSALM 139

Questions 1–3

Some people feel threatened by theological terms like *omniscience*, *omnipresence*, and *omnipotence*. They can seem foreign. But they are good words that capture rich meaning about who God is and what he does. Besides, when you break down the words, they really aren't so foreign and strange. The word "omni" really means "all." So, omnipresent simply means all-present.

For many of us, the idea that God knows everything, is everywhere, and can do anything is very comforting and helpful. Others don't like the idea at all ... it can feel intrusive, uncomfortable, like divine spying on their privacy. Be ready for a breadth of feelings when it comes to a discussion of these attributes of God. Hopefully, as we get the full picture and understand the love of God, his omniscience, omnipresence, and omnipotence should bring a sense of security and confidence to our lives.

Questions 4–6

David was somewhat overwhelmed when he wrote the first section of this psalm because he was aware of two unmistakable implications related to the subject of God's omniscience. First David pondered the reality, "If I have an omniscient God, this means that I am in relationship with someone even more wonderful than I ever dreamed." His second conclusion was, "If I am the object of such sovereign scrutiny, if his eyes are so fixed on me ... I must really matter to him. He doesn't scrutinize the trees like that. He doesn't get intimately acquainted with the ways of rocks and bushes. I am unique and valued in the eyes of my God."

Becoming personally aware of God's omniscience brings a healthy intrusion into our lives. We begin to think differently about what we think, say, and do. We stop trying to hide because we realize we can't hide anything from God. We begin confessing and seeking to change. As we see our lives the way they are—an open book before God—we desire transformation on a new level.

Questions 7–8

It's essential to catch the spirit of what David is saying in this next section of the psalm. If we miss this, we cut the heart out of Psalm 139. David is so astounded by the wonder and scope of God's care that he begins to imagine scenarios he knows are impossible. It is almost as if he is playing a game to find anywhere outside of God's loving embrace and caring hands.

Like a child, David asks his Father, "If I could go to the highest heaven or the deepest sea, will you be there? Will you still be holding my hand? What if I could sprout wings and fly across the farthest sea? Will your love still embrace me, Daddy? What if it is really, really, really dark and I am afraid? Will I be alone then?"

But David answers his own questions, because he knows! Because of God's omnipresent love and grace, there is no height, no depth, no ocean, no darkness that can separate us from his presence. In the New Testament the apostle Paul expresses it this way:

No, in all these things we are more than conquerors through him who loved us. For I am convinced that neither death nor life, neither angels nor demons, neither the present nor the future, nor any powers, neither height nor depth, nor anything else in all creation, will be able to separate us from the love of God that is in Christ Jesus our Lord. (Romans 8:37–39)

Questions 9–10

As David meditates on his own body, formed in his mother's womb by the hands of a loving God, he is overwhelmed. He cries out, "I am fearfully and wonderfully made!" I can just picture David reeling off a glorious list: "My eyes are optical marvels. My ears are physiological wonders. My skin, my sense of touch, and my sense of smell are amazing." And on and on.

When we stop to think of what God has done in making us, we realize that we are emotional, psychological, mental, and physical miracles. Each one of us has been custom designed by the Master Craftsman. We are not the result of some random selection of the natural world. We have been created by the hands of the supernatural God.

Group Reading:

For you created my inmost being;
    you knit me together in my mother's womb.
I praise you because I am fearfully and wonderfully
    made;
    your works are wonderful,
    I know that full well.
My frame was not hidden from you
    when I was made in the secret place.
When I was woven together in the depths of
    the earth,
    your eyes saw my unformed body.
All the days ordained for me
    were written in your book
    before one of them came to be.
How precious to me are your thoughts, O God!

cont.

How vast is the sum of them!
Were I to count them,
they would outnumber the grains of sand.
When I awake,
I am still with you. (Psalm 139:13–18)

Session Six – Worthy of Worship
PSALM 100

Question 1

Casual Christians and Comfortable Christians really aren't very dangerous. They pose no major threat to Satan. They offer little firepower for Christ or help to the local church. They don't have the energy to follow the leading of the Holy Spirit; they lack the devotion to give a sacrificial gift to the poor; they're not interested in adjusting their lifestyles to come in line with a biblical command. They are all about Christianity on their terms.

Some of these people will follow Jesus, as long as it doesn't upset the apple cart or cost them too much. They will show up for worship occasionally, but are more concerned about what they get than what they can give to God. At the end of the day, these people have embarrassingly little fulfillment in their faith or joy in their hearts. They just keep muddling along, calculating everything so they can invest as little as possible, while still doing their "religious duties."

Sadly, churches have plenty of Casual and Comfortable Christians. What we need are more Committed Christians who are ready to do anything for the sake of Jesus. A church with one hundred Committed Christians can do more for God than a church with one thousand Casual and Comfortable Christians.

Questions 2–3

There are so many attributes of God that lead Committed Christians to a place of deep worship. Psalm 100 points out specific characteristics and qualities such as:

- He is God.
- He is Creator.
- He is the Shepherd.
- He is good.

- He is a God of enduring love.
- He is faithful.

Each of these can direct our prayers, lead us to songs of praise, and move our hearts and lips to declare thanksgiving to him.

Questions 4–5

An honest study of the Bible will reveal a simple truth: Committed Christians who love God and walk in faithfulness still face times of pain, loss, and struggle. Examples are all over the Old and New Testaments and carry through the history of the church to our day. Yet Committed Christians discover that their joy and ability to worship God are based not on their circumstances, but on the unchanging nature of the One we worship.

When we become a community of worshipers who see the face of God in whatever the circumstance, joy overflows and gladness can't be restrained. This is not to say we never shed tears or have times of sorrow ... we do. But joy always wins the day. When the world looks at followers of Christ and the people of God gathered, they should see a relentless, unyielding joy.

Questions 6–7

The God of the Bible is the one true God. The world might not get this. There are even some scholars, professors, and pastors who claim to be Christians who might deny this, but it is exactly what the Bible teaches. As Christ followers we are in a relationship with the only true God by his grace through faith in Jesus. Because this is so, when we pray, our prayers are heard. When we call out for help, someone is home. When we worship, our worship is received, and our faith is well placed. Through the life, death, and resurrection of Jesus, by faith in his name, our eternal destiny is secure.

God is not a detached deity; he created us, knows each of us personally ... we matter to him. We are his people, the sheep of his pasture. It is as though the psalmist is saying, "In your wildest dreams we could never choose a better Shepherd. He loves us, watches over our lives, guides us, protects us, empowers us, fulfills us, comforts us, and provides all we need."

Questions 8–9

In verse 4 we are called to "enter his gates with thanksgiving," a reference to the thank offering. In our day this would be the equivalent of giving financial offerings to God's work. Just bring up this subject and Casual Christians get very quiet, even defensive. Comfortable Christians give minimally and reluctantly. They ask questions like, "Do I have to tithe the gross, or can I just tithe the net?" Or, "What do I *have* to give?" But Committed Christians open their hearts, hands, and bank accounts. They look for reasons to give and find joy in sharing with others.

If we find ourselves wondering, "What is the least I can get away with when it comes to giving?" it might be time to ask some other questions like:

- Has God saved me minimally?
- Has he cleansed me minimally?
- Has he gifted me minimally?
- Has he prepared a place for me in heaven that is second-rate?
- Has God poured out only a little love on me?

WILLOW
Willow Creek Association

Willow Creek Association
Vision, Training, Resources for Prevailing Churches

This resource was created to serve you and to help you build a local church that prevails. It is just one of many ministry tools that are part of the Willow Creek Resources® line, published by the Willow Creek Association together with Zondervan.

The Willow Creek Association (WCA) was created in 1992 to serve a rapidly growing number of churches from across the denominational spectrum that are committed to helping unchurched people become fully devoted followers of Christ. Membership in the WCA now numbers over 12,000 Member Churches worldwide from more than ninety denominations.

The Willow Creek Association links like-minded Christian leaders with each other and with strategic vision, training, and resources in order to help them build prevailing churches designed to reach their redemptive potential. Here are some of the ways the WCA does that.

- **The Leadership Summit**—a once a year, two-and-a-half-day conference to envision and equip Christians with leadership gifts and responsibilities. Presented live at Willow Creek as well as via satellite broadcast to over 130 locations across North America, this event is designed to increase the leadership effectiveness of pastors, ministry staff, volunteer church leaders, and Christians in the marketplace.

- **Ministry-Specific Conferences**—throughout each year the WCA hosts a variety of conferences and training events—both at Willow Creek's main campus and offsite, across the U.S., and around the world—targeting church leaders and volunteers in ministry-specific areas such as: small groups, preaching and teaching, the arts, children, students, volunteers, stewardship, etc.

- **Willow Creek Resources®**—provides churches with trusted and field-tested ministry resources in such areas as leadership, evangelism, spiritual formation, spiritual gifts, small groups, stewardship, student ministry, children's ministry, the use of the arts—drama, media, contemporary music—and more.

- **WCA Member Benefits**—includes substantial discounts to WCA training events, a 20 percent discount on all Willow Creek Resources®, *Defining Moments* monthly audio journal for leaders, quarterly *Willow* magazine, access to a Members-Only section on WillowNet, monthly communications, and more. Member Churches also receive special discounts and premier services through WCA's growing number of ministry partners—Select Service Providers—and save an average of $500 annually depending on the level of engagement.

For specific information about WCA conferences, resources, membership, and other ministry services contact:

Willow Creek Association
P.O. Box 3188
Barrington, IL 60011-3188
Phone: 847-570-9812
Fax: 847-765-5046
www.willowcreek.com

Just Walk Across the Room Curriculum Kit

Simple Steps Pointing People to Faith

Bill Hybels with *Ashley Wiersma*

In *Just Walk Across the Room*, Bill Hybels brings personal evangelism into the twenty-first century with a natural and empowering approach modeled after Jesus himself. When Christ "walked" clear across the cosmos more than 2,000 years ago, he had no forced formulas and no memorized script; rather, he came armed only with an offer of redemption for people like us, many of whom were neck-deep in pain of their own making.

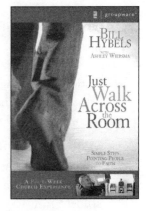

This dynamic four-week experience is designed to equip and inspire your entire church to participate in that same pattern of grace-giving by taking simple walks across rooms—leaving your circles of comfort and extending hands of care, compassion, and inclusiveness to people who might need a touch of God's love today.

Expanding on the principles set forth in Hybels' book of the same name, *Just Walk Across the Room* consists of three integrated components:

- Sermons, an implementation guide, and church promotional materials provided on CD-ROM to address the church as a whole
- Small group DVD and a participant's guide to enable people to work through the material in small, connected circles of community
- The book *Just Walk Across the Room* to allow participants to think through the concepts individually

Mixed Media Set: 978-0-310-27172-7

Pick up a copy at your favorite bookstore!

ZONDERVAN®
.com

When the Game Is Over,
It All Goes Back in the Box DVD

Six Sessions on Living Life in the Light of Eternity

John Ortberg with *Stephen* and
Amanda Sorenson

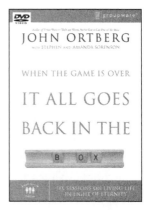

Using his humor and his genius for storytelling,
John Ortberg helps you focus on the real rules
of the game of life and how to set your priorities.
*When the Game Is Over, It All Goes Back in the
Box DVD* and participant's guide help explain
how, left to our own devices, we tend to seek out
worldly things, mistakenly thinking they will bring
us fulfillment. But everything on Earth belongs to
God. Everything we "own" is just on loan. And what
pleases God is often 180 degrees from what we may think is important.

In the six sessions you will learn how to:

- Live passionately and boldly
- Learn how to be active players in the game that pleases God
- Find your true mission and offer your best
- Fill each square on the board with what matters most
- Seek the richness of being instead of the richness of having

You can't beat the house, notes Ortberg. We're playing our game of life
on a giant board called a calendar. Time will always run out, so it's a good
thing to live a life that delights your Creator. When everything goes back in
the box, you'll have made what is temporary a servant to what is eternal, and
you'll leave this life knowing you've achieved the only victory that matters.

This DVD includes a 32-page leader's guide and is designed to be used
with the *When the Game Is Over, It All Goes Back in the Box* participant's
guide, which is available separately.

DVD-ROM: 978-0-310-28247-1
Participant's Guide: 978-0-310-28246-4

Pick up a copy at your favorite bookstore!

The Case for Christ DVD

A Six-Session Investigation of the Evidence for Jesus

Lee Strobel and *Garry Poole*

Is there credible evidence that Jesus of Nazareth really is the Son of God?

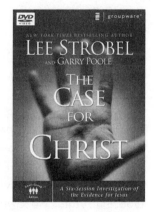

Retracing his own spiritual journey from atheism to faith, Lee Strobel, former legal editor of the *Chicago Tribune*, cross-examines several experts with doctorates from schools like Cambridge, Princeton, and Brandeis who are recognized authorities in their own fields.

Strobel challenges them with questions like:

- How reliable is the New Testament?
- Does evidence for Jesus exist outside the Bible?
- Is there any reason to believe the resurrection was an actual event?

Strobel's tough, point-blank questions make this six-session video study a captivating, fast-paced experience. But it's not fiction. It's a riveting quest for the truth about history's most compelling figure.

The six sessions include:

1. The Investigation of a Lifetime
2. Eyewitness Evidence
3. Evidence Outside the Bible
4. Analyzing Jesus
5. Evidence for the Resurrection
6. Reaching the Verdict

6 sessions; 1 DVD with leader's guide, 80 minutes (approximate).
The Case for Christ participant's guide is available separately.

DVD-ROM: 978-0-310-28280-8
Participant's Guide: 978-0-310-28282-2

The Case for a Creator DVD

A Six-Session Investigation of the Scientific Evidence That Points toward God

Lee Strobel and *Garry Poole*

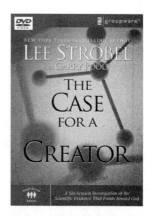

Former journalist and skeptic Lee Strobel has discovered something very interesting about science. Far from being the enemy of faith, science may now provide a solid foundation for believing in God.

Has science finally discovered God? Certainly new discoveries in such scientific disciplines as cosmology, cellular biology, astronomy, physics and DNA research are pointing to the incredible complexity of our universe, a complexity best explained by the existence of a Creator.

Written by Lee Strobel and Garry Poole, this six-session, 80-minute DVD curriculum comes with a companion participant's guide along with a leader's guide. The kit is based on Strobel's book and documentary *The Case for a Creator* and invites participants to encounter a diverse and impressive body of new scientific research that supports the belief in God. Weighty and complex evidence is delivered in a compelling conversational style.

The six sessions include:

1. Science and God
2. Doubts about Darwinism
3. The Evidence of Cosmology
4. The Fine-tuning of the Universe
5. The Evidence of Biochemistry
6. DNA and the Origin of Life

The Case for a Creator participant's guide is available separately.

DVD-ROM: 978-0-310-28283-9
Participant's Guide: 978-0-310-28285-3

The Case for Faith DVD

A Six-Session Investigation of the Toughest Objections to Christianity

Lee Strobel and *Garry Poole*

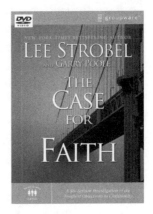

Doubt is familiar territory for Lee Strobel, the former atheist and award-winning author of books for skeptics and Christians. But he believes that faith and reason go hand in hand, and that Christianity is a defensible religion.

In this six-session video curriculum, Strobel uses his journalistic approach to explore the most common emotional obstacles to faith in Christ. These include the natural inclination to wrestle with faith and doubt, the troubling presence of evil and suffering in the world, and the exclusivity of the Christian gospel. They also include this compelling question: Can I doubt and be a Christian?

Through compelling video of personal stories and experts addressing these topics, combined with reflection and interaction, Christians and spiritual seekers will learn how to overcome these obstacles, deepen their spiritual convictions, and find new confidence that Christianity is a reasonable faith.

The Case for Faith participant's guide is available separately.

DVD-ROM: 978-0-310-24116-4
Participant's Guide: 978-0-310-24114-0

Pick up a copy at your favorite bookstore!

ReGroup™
Training Groups to Be Groups

Henry Cloud, Bill Donahue, and *John Townsend*

Whether you're a new or seasoned group leader, or whether your group is well-established or just getting started, the *ReGroup™* small group DVD and participant's guide will lead you and your group together to a remarkable new closeness and effectiveness. Designed to foster healthy group interaction and facilitate maximum growth, this innovative approach equips both group leaders and members with essential skills and values for creating and sustaining truly life-changing small groups. Created by three group life experts, the two DVDs in this kit include:

- Four sixty-minute sessions on the foundations of small groups that include teaching by the authors, creative segments, and activities and discussion time
- Thirteen five-minute coaching segments on topics such as active listening, personal sharing, giving and receiving feedback, prayer, calling out the best in others, and more

A participant's guide is sold separately.

DVD: 978-0-310-27783-5
Participant's Guide: 978-0-310-27785-9

Pick up a copy at your favorite bookstore!

ZONDERVAN®
.com

No Perfect People Allowed
(with 4-Week Church Experience DVD)

Creating a Come as You Are Culture in the Church

John Burke

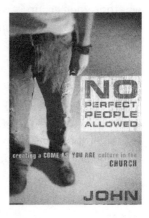

How do we live out the message of Jesus in today's ever-changing culture?

The church is facing its greatest challenge—and its greatest opportunity—in our postmodern, post-Christian world. God is drawing thousands of spiritually curious "imperfect people" to become his church—but how are we doing at welcoming them?

No Perfect People Allowed shows you how to deconstruct the five main barriers standing between emerging generations and your church by creating the right culture. From inspiring stories of real people once far from God, to practical ideas that can be applied by any local church, this book offers a refreshing vision of the potential and power of the body of Christ to transform lives today.

"We now are living in a post-Christian America—and that means we must be rethinking ministry through a missionary mindset. What makes this book both unique and extremely helpful is that it is filled with real-life stories of post-Christian people becoming followers of Jesus—not just statistics or data about them."

Dan Kimball, Author, *The Emerging Church*

"... John's 'get it' factor with people, lost or found, is something to behold! Reading this book filled me with optimism regarding the next generation of pastors and faith communities ..."

Bill Hybels, Senior Pastor, Willow Creek Community Church

"*No Perfect People Allowed* is a timely and necessary word for church leaders in a post-Christian culture. John Burke serves up quite a tasty meal full of the rich nutrients that will strengthen the body of Christ."

Randy Frazee, Senior Minister, Oak Hills Church;
Author, *The Connecting Church* and *Making Room for Life*

Hardcover, Jacketed: 978-0-310-27807-8

Share Your Thoughts

With the Author: Your comments will be forwarded to
the author when you send them to *zauthor@zondervan.com*.

With Zondervan: Submit your review of this book
by writing to *zreview@zondervan.com*.

Free Online Resources at
www.zondervan.com/hello

 Zondervan AuthorTracker: Be notified whenever your
favorite authors publish new books, go on tour, or post
an update about what's happening in their lives.

 Daily Bible Verses and Devotions: Enrich your life
with daily Bible verses or devotions that help you start
every morning focused on God.

 Free Email Publications: Sign up for newsletters on
fiction, Christian living, church ministry, parenting, and
more.

 Zondervan Bible Search: Find and compare
Bible passages in a variety of translations at
www.zondervanbiblesearch.com.

 Other Benefits: Register yourself to receive online
benefits like coupons and special offers, or to participate
in research.